ISBN 0 85116 195 2

The
Fireside Book

A picture and a poem
for every mood
chosen by

David Hope

Printed and Published by
D. C. THOMSON & CO. LTD.
185 Fleet Street, LONDON EC4A 2HS

ENGLAND'S WEATHER

WHO can say what an English day
    Will be in the space of an hour?
For the frozen guise of the winter skies
Can dissolve in an April shower.

On a day in June it can pour at noon
From a sky where no cloudlet lay,
While a mocking breeze in the Christmas trees
Plays a springtime roundelay.

At its distant birth the Lord gave Earth
A clime for ever nation;
But England was missed from the Weather
    Clerk's list
In the heavenly dispensation.

So the Arctic zone and the monsoon's moan,
With the heat of the desert waste,
Were blended together, producing the
    weather
That suits our English taste.

So we never complain of incessant rain
Or heat-waves or frost all the time.
Our weather-report is a variable sort,
And change is the charm of our clime.

Noel Scott

WHEN BEAUTY COMES

WHEN Beauty comes,
    Then see!
For fear she pass
From thee,
As petals blow to grass.

When music comes,
Then hear!
Lest it depart
In fear
Of your unanswering heart.

If love should come,
(Ah hist!
And whisper low!)
Unkissed,
He too may turn and go.

K. V. Chevis

THE ADVENTURER

I'VE hunted treasure,
  Been a buccaneer,
An exiled monarch
And a famous spy;
I've climbed Mount Everest,
And seen the sun
With blazing fingers
Paint the morning sky.
I've journeyed round the world
A score of times,
I've roamed the countryside
And tramped the town
In search of work,
A roaming vagabond—
And on a fragrant hayrick
Laid me down
To sleep beneath High Heaven's spangled dome,
And yet—to travel—I have ne'er left home.
I use Imagination's fiery steed
That's stabled in the books I love to read!

Aileen E. Passmore

THE SOUTH COUNTRY

WHEN I am living in the Midlands
　　That are sodden and unkind,
I light my lamp in the evening:
　　My work is left behind;
And the great hills of the South Country
　　Come back into my mind.

The great hills of the South Country
　　They stand along the sea;
And it's there walking in the high woods
　　That I could wish to be,
And the men that were boys when I was a boy
　　Walking along with me.

I never get between the pines
　　But I smell the Sussex air;
Nor I never come on a belt of sand
　　But my home is there.
And along the sky the line of the Downs
　　So noble and so bare.

If I ever become a rich man,
   Or if ever I grow to be old,
I will build a house with deep thatch
   To shelter me from the cold,
And there shall the Sussex songs be sung
   And the story of Sussex told.

I will hold my house in the high wood
   Within a walk of the sea,
And the men that were boys when I was a boy
   Shall sit and drink with me.

Hilaire Belloc

NOVEMBER BLUE

A HEAVENLY colour, London town
    Has blurred it from her skies;
And, hooded in an earthly brown,
    Unheaven'd the city lies.
No longer, standard-like, this hue
    Above the broad road flies;
Nor does the narrow street the blue
    Wear, slender pennon-wise.

But when the gold and silver lamps
    Colour the London dew,
And misted by the winter damps,
    The shops shine bright anew—
Blue comes to earth, it walks the street,
    It dyes the wide air through;
A mimic sky about their feet,
    The throng go crowned with blue.

Alice Meynell

FARM HOMES

I LIKE a kitchen big enough
   To hold a rocking chair,
With windows looking to the sun,
   And flowers blooming there.
I like big cupboards by the wall
   That hold a lot of things,
The cups hung up on little hooks,
   A yellow bird that sings.

I like to do my mending there,
   Where I can watch the road,
And see the teams come plodding home,
   And smell their fragrant load
Of heavy sheaves at stacking time,
   Or hear the wagons creak
And groan beneath their golden weight,
   If it is threshing week.

I like to have the supper on,
   And let it simmer slow,
With rich brown gravy bubbling up
   Around the meat, you know.
With apple pie set out to cool
   And flaky new baked bread,
With golden syrup in a bowl
   And jelly warm and red.

I like to have the lamps ashine,
   With yellow glowing light,
And have the kitchen warm and clean
   When they come in at night.
To make a home so snug and dear,
   That when they work or play,
They hold a picture in their hearts
   Of home, at close of day.

Edna Jaques

THE TRAVELLER'S RETURN

SWEET to the morning traveller
   The song amid the sky,
Where, twinkling in the dewy light,
   The skylark soars on high.

And cheering to the traveller
   The gales that round him play,
When faint and heavily he drags
   Along his noontide way.

And when beneath the unclouded sun
   Full wearily toils he,
The flowing water makes to him
   A soothing melody.

And when the evening light decays,
   And all is calm around,
There is sweet music to his ear
   In the distant sheep-bells' sound.

But oh! of all beautiful sounds
   Of evening or of morn,
The sweetest is the voice of love
   That welcomes his return.

Robert Southey

IS LIFE WORTH LIVING?

IS life worth living? Yes, so long
   As Spring revives the year,
And hails us with the cuckoo's song,
   To show that she is here;
So long as May of April takes,
   In smiles and tears, farewell,
And windflowers dapple all the brakes,
   And primroses in the dell;
While children in the woodlands yet
   Adorn their little laps
With ladysmock and violet,
   And daisy-chain their caps;
While over orchard daffodils
   Cloud-shadows float and fleet,
And ousel pipes and laverock trills
   And young lambs buck and bleat;
So long as that which bursts the bud
   And swells and tunes the rill,
Makes springtime in the maiden's blood,
   Life is worth living still.

Alfred Austin

THE GOLFER

MY days upon the links are pass'd,
   Around me I behold,
Where'er my visual orbs are cast,
   What I prize more than gold:
O 'tis magnificent, methinks,
Thrice daily to play round the links!

Thereto at early dawn I steal
   In sunshine, gale, or snow;
And glorious 'tis in form to feel,
   When drives like rockets go,
Approaches reach the destined goal,
And long putts seldom miss the hole.

Feeble and tame is any fire,
   Tho' on petroleum fed,
Compared with my intense desire
   The velvet turf to tread,
To watch the sea, and breathe the wind,
Leaving all earthly care behind.

My hopes are on the links: perhaps
   To me a prize may fall
In spite of pressing or a lapse
   Very occasional—
And, if I win a cup, I trust
It will not, being base metal, rust!

S. Raleigh Simpson

COMMUNION

At the waking of birds,
  In the hush of morning,
We whisper the words
  Of praise and repentance;
The sun from the East
  Stains pillar and chancel,
The voice of the priest
  Comes soft-toned and solemn;
And out in the world
  The first dews are trampled,
The dawn-mists are furled,
  The cows go from milking,
A cock crows loud
  From the farmyard midden;
But here in a cloud
  Of worship and silence
We keep the old tryst,
  We serve the commandment
Of Jesus the Christ;
  Desiring, receiving—
To the carol of birds,
  In the world just waking—
The comfortable words
  Of Jesus the Saviour.

P. B. H. Lyon

THE TAKEOVER

PUSS was hungry and thin when she came to
  my door
  On a bitterly cold winter's night.
"What, all on your lonesome?" she seemed to
  be saying,
  "That's something we'll have to put right.
I'd be pleased to accept just a morsel to eat
  Of whatever you feel you can spare.
Yes, a tin of sardines will do nicely for me,
  Then I fancy a doze in your chair.
No, I'll not be a nuisance or make any fuss
  And I won't crowd you out of the house,
But just now and then I shall make you a gift
  Of a dear little very dead mouse."
Now I've three pretty kittens the image of Puss
  Right down to the very last paw.
If you really don't want to be owned by a cat,
  Then you'd better not answer the door!

Irene Bernaerts

THE MILLER'S SONG

FULL many a night in the clear moonlight
   Have I wandered by valley and down,
Where owls fly low, and hoot as they go—
   The white-wing'd owl, and the brown.
For it's up and away ere the dawn of the day,
   When the glow-worm shines in the grasses,
And the dusk lies cool on the reed-set pool,
   And the night wind passes.

Full many a day have I found my way
   Where the long road winds round the hill,
Where the wind blows free, on a juniper lea,
   To the tune and the clank of a mill.
For the miller's a man who must work while he can
   With the rye, and the barley growing,
While the slow wheels churn, and the great sails turn,
   To the fresh wind, blowing.

Pamela Tennant

THE DEVOUT ANGLER

THE years will bring their anodyne
   But I shall never quite forget
The fish that I had counted mine
    And lost before they reached the net.

Last night I put my rod away
   Remorseful and disconsolate,
Yet I had suffered yesterday
   No more than I deserved from fate.

And as I scored another trout
   Upon my list of fish uncaught,
I should have offered thanks, no doubt,
   For salutary lessons taught.

Alas! Philosophy avails
   As little as it used to do:
More comfort is there still in tales
   That may be, or may not be true.

When in my pilgrimage I reach
   The river that we all must cross,
And land upon that further beach
   Where earthly gains are counted loss,

May I not earthly loss repair?
   Well, if those fish should rise again,
There shall be no more parting there—
   Celestial gut will stand the strain.

And, issuing from the portal, one
   Who was himself a fisherman
Will drop his Keys and, shouting, run
   To help me land leviathan!

Colin D. B. Ellis

WINTER SUNRISE

YELLOW jasmine, delicate on stiff branches
        Stands in a Tuscan pot to delight the eye
In spare December's patient nakedness.

Suddenly, softly, as if at a breath breathed
On the pale wall, a magical apparition,
The shadow of jasmine, branch and blossom!

It was not there, it is there, in a perfect image;
And all is changed. It is like a memory lost
Returning without a reason into the mind;

And it seems to me that the beauty of the shadow
Is more beautiful than the flower; a strange
        beauty,
Pencilled and silently deepening to distinctness;

As a memory stealing out of the mind's slumber,
A memory floating up from a dark water,
Can be more beautiful than the thing remembered.

                    Laurence Binyon

AT EUSTON

STRANGER with the pile of luggage, proudly
   labelled for Portree,
How I wish this night of August I were you and
   you were me!
Think of all that lies before you when the train
   goes sliding forth,
And the lines athwart the sunset lead you swiftly
   to the North.

Think of breakfast at Kingussie, think of high
   Drumochter Pass,
Think of Highland breezes singing through the
   bracken and the grass.
Scabious blue and yellow daisy, tender fern
   beside the train,
Rowdy Tummel, falling, brawling, seen and lost,
   and glimpsed again.

You will pass my golden roadway of the days
  of long ago.
Will you realise the magic of the names I used
  to know,
Clachnaharry, Achnashellach, Achnasheen and
  Duirinish?
Every moor alive with coveys, every pool aboil
  with fish.

Every well-remembered vista, more exciting mile
  by mile,
Till the wheeling gulls are screaming round the
  engine at the Kyle.
Think of cloud on Bheinn na Cailleach, jagged
  Cuillin soaring high,
Scent of peat, and all the glamour of the misty
  Isle of Skye.

A.M. Harbord

JUST LIKE A MAN

HE sat at the dinner table
    With a discontented frown,
The potatoes and steak were underdone
    And the bread was baked too brown;
The pie was too sour and the pudding too sweet,
    And the roast was much too fat;
The soup so greasy, too, and salt,
    'Twas hardly fit for the cat.

" I wish you could eat the bread and pie
    I've seen my mother make,
They are something like, and 'twould do you good
    Just to look at a loaf of her cake."
Said the smiling wife, " I'll improve with age—
    Just now I'm but a beginner;
But your mother has come to visit us,
    And today she cooked the dinner."

Anon.

TEWKESBURY ROAD

IT is good to be out on the road, and going one
    knows not where,
Going through meadow and village, one knows
    not whither or why;
Through the grey light drift of the dust, in the keen
    cool rush of the air,
Under the flying white clouds, and the broad blue
    lift of the sky;

And to halt at the chattering brook, in the tall
    green fern at the brink,
Where the harebell grows, and the gorse, and the
    foxgloves purple and white;
Where the shy-eyed delicate deer troop down to
    the pools to drink
When the stars are mellow and large at the
    coming on of the night.

O, to feel the warmth of the rain, and the homely
    smell of the earth,
Is a tune for the blood to jig to, a joy past power
    of words;
And the blessed green comely meadows seem all
    a-ripple with mirth
At the lilt of the shifting feet and the dear wild cry
    of the birds.

John Masefield

THE NIGHTINGALE

THE speckled bird sings in the tree
  When all the stars are silver-pale.
Come, children, walk the night with me,
  And we shall hear the nightingale.

The nightingale is a shy bird,
  He flits before you through the night.
And now the sleepy vale is stirred
  Through all its green and gold and white.

The blackbird turns upon his bed,
  The thrush has oped a sleeping eye,
Quiet each downy sleepy-head;
  But who goes singing up the sky?

It is, it is the nightingale,
  In the tall tree upon the hill.
To moonlight and the dewy vale
  The nightingale will sing his fill.

He's but a homely, speckled bird,
  But he has gotten a golden flute,
And when his wondrous song is heard,
  Blackbird and thrush and lark are mute.

Troop, children, dear, out to the night,
  Clad in the moonlight silver-pale,
And in a world of green and white
  'Tis you shall hear the nightingale.

Katharine Tynan

WISHES

I WISH I liked rice pudding,
  I wish I were a twin,
I wish some day a real live fairy
    Would just come walking in.

I wish when I'm at table
  My feet would touch the floor,
I wish our pipes would burst next winter,
  Just like they did next door.

I wish that I could whistle
  Real proper grown-up tunes,
I wish they'd let me sweep the chimneys
  On rainy afternoons.

I've got such heaps of wishes,
  I've only said a few;
I wish that I could wake some morning
  And find they'd all come true!

Rose Fyleman

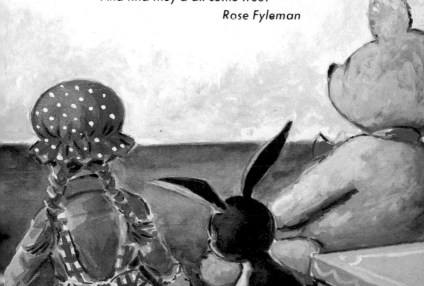

A DROVER

TO Meath of the pastures,
    From wet hills by the sea,
Through Leitrim and Longford,
    Go my cattle and me.

I hear in the darkness
    Their slipping and breathing—
I name them the bye-ways
    They're to pass without heeding;

Then the wet, winding roads,
    Brown bogs with black water;
And my thoughts on white ships
    And the King o' Spain's daughter.

O! farmer, strong farmer!
    You can spend at the fair;
But your face you must turn
    To your crops and your care.

O! the smell of the beasts,
    The wet wind in the morn;
And the proud and hard earth
    Never broken for corn;

And the crowds at the fair,
    The herds loosened and blind,
Loud words and dark faces
    And the wild blood behind.

I will bring you, my kine,
    Where there's grass to the knee;
But you'll think of scant croppings
    Harsh with salt of the sea.

Padraic Colum

THE LANE

BEYOND this lane's luminous eve
　　Where linnet and tired blackbird weave
Traceries of enchanted air,
Where lovers glimpsed at unaware
Snatch kisses from the fading day,
Where wistfully, as far away,
A cuckoo's note is loosed and furled
Stretch all the highways of the world.
There, I have heard, that tides are fleet,
That men on restless, flame-like feet
Tread cities that are ageless old;
Wing through the air, and trek for gold,
Following through the seven seas
Their far desires and destinies.

Yet still it seems this lane holds all
The fluttering leaves of evenfall;
The singing field where grasses stir
Slight scabious pale as lavender,
Where sorrel and red poppy keep
A drowsy charm to conjure sleep,
Is all that I shall ever know
Of men that roam and tides that flow.
There is no road, no boundless sea,
No continents immensity
Beyond this lane that cradles me.

K. V. Chevis

THE DREAMER

OH, London Strand, 'tis all a-hum
    And thronged with wheels and men,
But I would slack till kingdom come
    And never touch a pen,
For I am fresh caught from the spells,
    That haunt the home of deer,
And I have heard the heather bells
    That sound so small and clear.

Oh, London Strand's a sounding-shore,
    Laborious and murk,
Yet I would idle evermore
    And never set to work,
For I have drunk of days that shone,
    That fast, as grouse-packs, flew,
And looked, mayhap too often, on
    The hills when they were blue.

Patrick R. Chalmers

THE SHEPHERDESS

SHE walks — the lady of my delight —
   A shepherdess of sheep.
Her flocks are thoughts. She keeps them white;
   She guards them from the steep;
She feeds them on the fragrant height,
   And folds them in for sleep.

She roams maternal hills and bright,
   Dark valleys safe and deep.
Into that tender breast at night the chastest stars
    may peep.
She walks — the lady of my delight —
   A shepherdess of sheep.

She holds her little thoughts in sight,
   Though gay they run and leap.
She is so circumspect and right;
   She has her soul to keep.
She walks — the lady of my delight —
   A shepherdess of sheep.

Alice Meynell

SONG OF HONOUR

I CLIMBED a hill as light fell short,
  And rooks came home in scramble sort,
And filled the trees and flapped and fought
And sang themselves to sleep.
An owl from nowhere with no sound
Swung by and soon was nowhere found,
I heard him calling half-way round,
  Holloing loud and deep.
A pair of stars, faint pins of light,
Then many a star, sailed into sight,
And all the stars, the flower of night,
  Were round me at a leap.
To tell how still the valleys lay,
I heard a watch-dog miles away,
  And bells of distant sheep.

I heard no more of bird or bell,
The mastiff in a slumber fell,
  I stared into the sky,
As wondering men have always done
Since beauty and the stars were one,
  Though none so hard as I.

It seemed, so still the valleys were,
As if the whole world knelt at prayer,
  Save me and me alone;
So pure and wide that silence was
I feared to bend a blade of grass,
  And there I stood like stone.

Ralph Hodgson

THE OLD LOVE

OUT of my door I step into
  The country, all her scent and dew,
Nor travel there by a hard road,
Dusty and far from my abode.

The country washes to my door
Green miles on miles in soft uproar,
The thunder of the woods, and then
The backwash of green surf again.

Beyond the feverfew and stocks,
The guelder-rose and hollyhocks;
Outside my trellised porch a tree
Of lilac frames a sky for me.

The country silence wraps me quite,
Silence and song and pure delight;
The country beckons all the day
Smiling, and but a step away.

This is that country seen across
How many a league of love and loss,
Prayed for and longed for, and as far
As fountains in the desert are.

This is that country at my door,
Whose fragrant airs run on before,
And call me when the first birds stir
In the green wood to walk with her.

Katharine Tynan

MAY SONG

As I rode o'er the dunes today
   I heard the peewits cry;
Their nests were in the whistling sedge
That clothed the links from edge to edge
   And streamed to meet the sky.

The sun was on the world today
  As I went riding by,
All silken was the rippling lea,
Satin and lace the tumbling sea
  Under a ribboned sky.

We raced across the sands today,
  My chestnut colt and I;
And flying hoofs and singing sea
And all the glad wind's minstrelsy
  Chimed to the lark-loud sky.

Dorothy Margaret Paulin

YEOMEN OF SOMERSET

MY sons will love these solemn woods
    And red fields scarred beneath the plough,
Their hands will latch these gates, their feet
Will tread the lanes I pass through now;
My sons will learn to stand and gaze
At swallow's dip and heron's flight,
And, staring at the ancient stars
Praise God on every frosty night.

And yet, must I go hence someday—
Leave them to reap where I have sown,
Desert these dear, familiar streams
And cherished meads? . . . One thought alone
Brings solace to my rebel heart—
My fathers watched with loving eyes
The fathers of these same black rooks
Tilting against these same blue skies.

Joyce E. J. Collard

THE HARVEST MOON

THE crimson Moon, uprising from the sea,
　　With large delight foretells the harvest near:
Ye shepherds, now prepare your melody
　　To greet the soft appearance of her sphere;
And, like a page enamoured of her train,
　　The star of evening glimmers in the west:
Then raise, ye shepherds, your observant strain,
　　That so of the Great Shepherd here are blest.
Our fields are full with the time-ripened grain,
　　Our vineyards with the purple clusters swell;
Her golden splendour glimmers on the main,
　　And vales and mountains her bright glory tell:
Then sing, ye shepherds, for the time is come
　　When we must bring the enriched harvest home.

Edward Hovel, Lord Thurlow

WHEN WE ARE SAD

WHEN we are sad
    The small things are our friends:
A lamplit window
When the long day ends;
A kettle singing;
Wallflowers drenched with dew;
The old clock ticking,
And the friendly blue
Of willow-pattern
In a kitchen bright;
A kitten purring
By the fire; the flight
Of birds across the tree-tops;
Butterflies.
When we are sad, ah then,
Ah then we're wise
With a new wisdom,
And we realise
The goodness in all things,
And thank God, who sends
The comforting small things
To be our friends!

Aileen E. Passmore

MY LOVE

I'LL weave my love a garland,
  He shall be dressed so fine.
I'll set it round with roses,
  With lilies, pinks, and thyme;
And I'll present it to my love
  When he comes back from sea:
For I love my love, and I love my love
  Because my love loves me.

I wish I were an arrow
  That sped into the air,
To seek him as a sparrow,
  And if he be not there
Then quickly I'd become a fish
  To search the raging sea:
For I love my love, and I love my love
  Because my love loves me.

I would I were a reaper,
  I'd seek him in the corn;
I would I were a keeper,
  I'd hunt him with my horn;
I'd blow a blast, when found at last,
  Beneath the greenwood tree:
For I love my love, and I love my love,
  Because my love loves me.

                    Anon.

JULY

THE wind is in the willows, they are white
    beneath the breeze,
  And the river rushes rustle as they grow.
The skimming swifts and swallows dip and sweep
    beneath the trees,
  Where the white-flowered water-weeds blow.
At the foot of leaning poplars bowing grey against
    the blue,
  The quiet sheep are feeding newly shorn,
And among the standing barley, shot with
    poppies, through and through,
  The land-rail is craking in the corn.

All day the doves are calling, and the rose is on
    the hedge,
  Where the black-berried bryonies stray,
The yellow flower-de-luce is growing tall among
    the sedge,
  Where the clover was crimson in the hay.
O, the sounds and scents of summer blowing free
    upon the breeze!
  The honeysuckle fashioned like a horn,
And the fragrance of the elder, in a dusk of
    stirring trees,
  And the night-jar churring on the thorn.

Pamela Tennant

SO PLEASANT IT IS TO HAVE MONEY

AS I sat at the cafe, I said to myself,
    They may talk as they please about what they
      call pelf,
They may sneer as they like about eating and
    drinking,
But help it I cannot, I cannot help thinking
    How pleasant it is to have money, heigh ho!
    How pleasant it is to have money.

We sit at our tables and tipple champagne;
Ere one bottle goes, comes another again;
The waiters they skip and they scuttle about,
And the landlord attends us so civilly out.
    So pleasant it is to have money, heigh ho!
    So pleasant it is to have money.

It was but last winter I came up to town,
But already I'm getting a little renown;
I get to good houses without much ado,
Am beginning to see the nobility too.
    So pleasant it is to have money, heigh ho!
    So pleasant it is to have money.

O dear! what a pity they ever should lose it!
For they are the gentry that know how to use it;
So grand and so graceful, such manners, such
    dinners
But yet, after all, it is we are the winners.
    So pleasant it is to have money, heigh ho!
    So pleasant it is to have money.

Arthur Hugh Clough

THE HOUSE OF DREAMS

WILL make you a little house with a roof of
    thatch,
  And a window as clear as crystal dew, and a door
With a knocker of pearl, and a silver dream for a
    latch,
  And a carpet of little blue feathers to lay on your
    floor.

And your bed shall be rocked by the music of wind
    and of sea,
  And your fire be lit by the daffodil light of Spring;
And high on the shining wall of your house shall be
  The Bird of Joy in an ivory cage to sing.

Never a sorrow shall enter, and never pain,
  Never the sorrowful cry of the wind shall fret
Or your heart be sad or your eyes be dim again:
  Sleep, O my Heart of Gold, sleep and forget.

Thora Stowell

MY DELIGHT AND THY DELIGHT

MY delight and thy delight
   Walking, like two angels white,
In the gardens of the night:

My desire and thy desire
Twining to a tongue of fire,
Leaping live, and laughing higher;
Thro' the everlasting strife
In the mystery of life.

Love, from whom the world begun,
Hath the secret of the sun.

Love can tell, and love alone,
Whence the million stars were strewn,
Why each atom knows its own,
How, in spite of woe and death,
Gay is life, and sweet is breath:

This he taught us, this we knew,
Happy in his science true,
Hand in hand as we stood
Neath the shadows of the wood,
Heart to heart as we lay
In the dawning of the day.

Robert Bridges

HELFORD RIVER

HELFORD RIVER, Helford River,
　　Blessed may ye be!
We sailed up Helford River
　　By Durgan from the sea.

O to hear the hawser chain
　　Rattle by the ferry there!
Dear, and shall we come again
　　　　By Bosahan,
　By wood and water fair?

All the wood to ransack,
　　All the wave explore—
Moon on Calamansack,
　　Ripple on the shore.

Laid asleep and dreaming
　　On our cabin beds;
Helford River streaming
　　By two happy heads;

Helford river, streaming
　　By Durgan to the sea,
Much have we been dreaming
　　Since we dreamed by thee.

Dear, and shall we dream again
　　The one dream there?
All may go if that remain
　　　　By Bosahan,
And the old face wear!

Sir A. T. Quiller-Couch

THE GARDEN

NOT wholly in the busy world, nor quite
    Beyond it, blooms the garden that I love.
News from the humming city comes to it
In sound of funeral or of marriage bells;
And, sitting muffled in dark leaves, you hear
The windy clanging of the minster clock;
Although between it and the garden lies
A league of grass, wash'd by a slow broad
    stream,
That, stirr'd with languid pulses of the oar,
Waves all its lazy lilies, and creeps on,
Barge-laden, to three arches of a bridge
Crown'd with the minster-towers. The fields
    between
Are dewy-fresh, browsed by deep-uddered kine,
And all about the large lime feathers low,
The lime a summer home of murmurous wings.

Alfred, Lord Tennyson

MEETING AT NIGHT

THE grey sea and the long black land;
 And the yellow half-moon large and low;
And the startled little waves that leap
In fiery ringlets from their sleep,
As I gain the cove with pushing prow,
And quench its speed in the slushy sand.

Then a mile of warm sea-scented beach;
Three fields to cross till a farm appears;
A tap at the pane, the quick sharp scratch
And blue spurt of a lighted match,
And a voice less loud, thro' its joys and fears,
Than the two hearts beating each to each!

Robert Browning

WIZARDS

THERE'S many a proud wizard from Araby to
  Egypt
Can read the silver writing of the stars as they run;
And many a dark gipsy, with a pheasant in his
  knapsack
Has gathered more by moonshine than wiser
  men have won;
    But I know a wizardry
    Can take a buried acorn,
And whisper forests out of it, to tower against the
  sun.

There's many a magician, from Bagdad to
  Benares,
Can read you for a penny what your future is to be;
And a flock of crazy prophets that by staring in
  a crystal
Can fill it with more fancies than there's herring
  in the sea;
    But I know a wizardry
    Can take a freckled egg-shell,
And shake a throstle out of it in every hawthorn
  tree.

There's many a crafty alchemist from Mecca to
  Jerusalem,
And Michael Scott and Merlin were reckoned
  very wise;
But I know a wizardry can take a wisp of sun-fire
And round it to a planet, and roll it through
  the skies,
    With cities, and sea-ports,
    And little shining windows,
And hedge-rows, and gardens, and loving human
  eyes.

Alfred Noyes

THE WINTER TREE

WHEN I shall come to set my face
   Unto the vast of farther space,
When with my final beat of time
I needs must seek the far sublime,
May it be mine ahead to see,
Against the new-dawn jewelry,
The tracery of the winter tree.

My spirit shall take wings and soar,
Nor see the reeling starry floor,
If cool and clean—refreshment rare—
I glimpse fine-etched on limpid air,
Beech, ash, elm, lime, birch, poplar tall,
Oak, willow, hawthorn's mazy scrawl—
No matter which, or one, or all.

                    John S. Martin

LAMP LIGHT

YOUR love is the lamp
    That lights my way,
Transfiguring
Each humdrum day,
Scattering shadows and ghosts of fears,
Bringing laughter, dispelling tears.

Your love is the fire
That warms my room,
Vanquishing
All trace of gloom,
Kindly comfort that will abide,
Secure against the storms outside.

Your love is the flame
That will not die,
Unquenched as time
Hurries by;
We shared our lives and you came to be
The radiant hope in the heart of me.

Frances Stephens

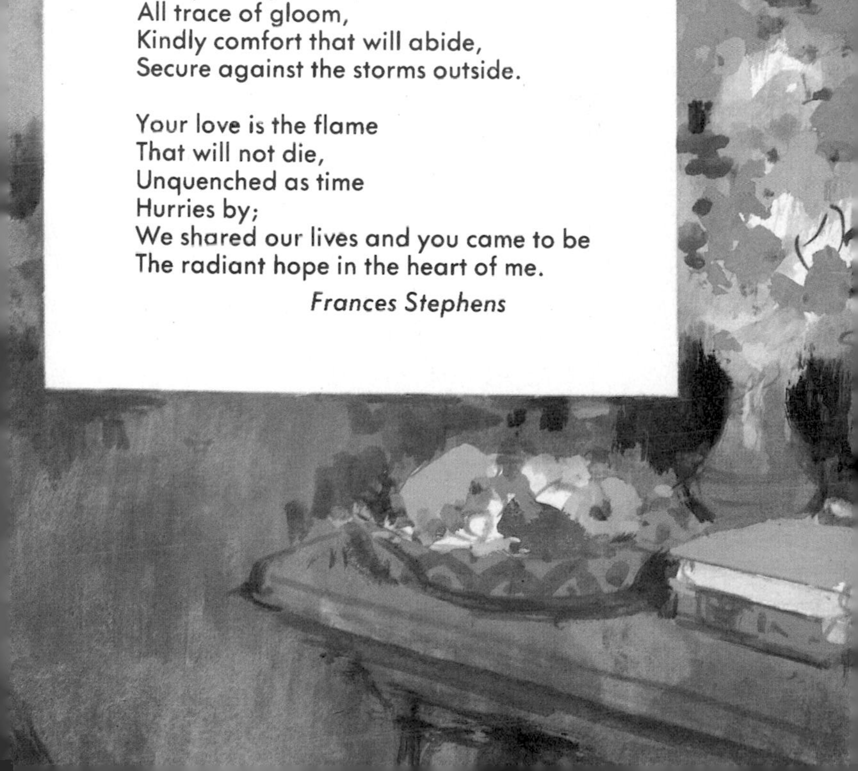

WILL YOU?

WILL you take my hand and walk with me
    Through my dark nights and bright clear
      days,
Will you be with me?

Can you sit with me, content, but stand
Fast and calm when searing winds
Sing bitter songs for us?

Will you stay with me through golden years,
Watching our children's happy dreams
Take root and grow?

Will you love me till Time's shadow falls
Softly across our smiling hearts,
And o'er our sun?

Pat Lovell

THE TORTOISESHELL CAT

THE tortoiseshell cat
    She sits on the mat,
As gay as a sunflower she;
    In orange and black you see her blink,
    And her waistcoat's white, and her nose is pink,
And her eyes are green of the sea.
    But all is vanity, all the way;
    Twilight's coming and close of day,
    And every cat in the twilight's grey,
        Every possible cat.

The tortoiseshell cat
    She is smooth and fat,
And we call her Josephine,
    Because she weareth upon her back
    This coat of colours, this raven black,
This red of the tangerine.
    But all is vanity, all the way;
    Twilight follows the brightest day,
    And every cat in the twilight's grey,
        Every possible cat.

Patrick R. Chalmers

THE TRINKET BOX

THE trinket box came down to me
　　From Grandmama when I was three.
She told me of the treasures there,
Very old, beyond compare:

Dainty earrings, gleaming gold,
They came from Paris, I was told,
This serpent bracelet of beaten brass,
Was found in a market in old Madras;

A string of pearly necklace beads,
Those finer ones that look like seeds;
A heart-shaped brooch, a cross and chain,
And crystal drops that look like rain.

All these treasures that glint and shine
Were once Grandma's, but now they're mine.
I don't suppose I'll ever know
How much they're worth; but this I know,
They're more to me than the wealth of kings
Because they were my Grandma's things.

Glenda Moore

HOW MANY TIMES?

HOW many times do I love thee, dear?
Tell me how many thoughts there be
In the atmosphere
Of the new fall'n year,
Whose white and sable hours appear
The latest flake of eternity:
So many times do I love thee, dear!

How many times do I love again?
Tell me how many beads there are
In a silver chain
Of evening rain
Unravelled from the tumbling main,
And threading the eye of a yellow star:
So many times do I love again!

Thomas Lovell Beddoes

A WINTER EVENING

AT night outside my window there's a rush and
    whirr of wings,
As if the trees and hedges and all insensate things
Were struggling in their slumber to reach the time
    that brings
The glamour and the wonder and gladness of new
    Springs.

The mystic sounds of night-time, the creak of home-
    ward carts,
The whistling of a drover, the beat of hidden
    hearts,
The birth-cry of a baby who on life's journey
    starts—
The sobs of lonely mourners as some loved soul
    departs.

The warmth and glow of night-time, with doors
    and windows tight,
In dressing-gown and slippers, the old dog well in
    sight,
The favourite book, the fireside—oh, comfort and
    delight!
Indeed what is more peaceful than a shut-in
    Winter's night?

And yet, outside my window seems to come the
    whirr of wings,
As if to stir my being with desire for other things—
With yearning for the promise that pulsing
    morrow brings,
The enchantment and the rapture, the fulfilment of
    new Springs!

Caroline Russell Bispham

FIRST LOVE

GIVE me your hand! The evening air is still,
  And the first stars are hungering for the
  night.
Above the trees the moon slips into light
Golden and large. Let us go on until
She stands above us small and silver-white,
And washes every shadow from the hill.
Let us go on! Dear, let us dream no ill
Of one another with the stars in sight.
Let us forget the world and all we know
Of dark distrust, since love has laid her spell
Upon our hearts, miraculous and clear.
There may be worlds where thoughts of beauty
  flow
Unquestioned, unpolluted. Can we tell
How often God may speak before we hear?

K. V. Chevis

THE CARAVAN

IF I could be a gipsy-boy and have a caravan
  I'd travel all the world, I would, before I was
    a man;
We'd drive beyond the far blue hills—us two, my
  horse and me—
And on and on and on and on until we reached
  the sea.

And there I'd wash his legs quite clean and bid him
  come inside,
Whilst I would stand upon the roof and scan the
  flowing tide,
And he and I would sail away and scorn the
  Spanish main,
And when we'd swept the Spaniards out we'd
  p'r'aps sail home again.

Or if my horse was very tired of ships and being
  good,
And wanted most to stretch his legs (as many
  horses would),
We'd call a whale to tow us to a desert island
  beach,
And there we'd search for coconuts and have a
  whole one each.

If I could be a gipsy boy I wouldn't bring a load
Of pots and pans and chairs and things and sell
  them in the road.
Oh, if I was a gipsy boy and had a caravan
I'd see the whole wide world, I would, before I
  was a man.

Madeleine Nightingale

THE WEST WIND

IT'S a warm wind, the west wind, full of birds' cries;
　I never hear the west wind but tears are in my eyes.
For it comes from the west lands, the old brown hills,
And April's in the west wind, and daffodils.

It's a fine land, the west land, for hearts as tired as mine,
Apple orchards blossom there, and the air's like wine.
There is cool green grass there, where men may lie at rest.
And the thrushes are in song there, fluting from
　　the nest.

'Will ye not come home, brother? Ye have been long
　　away,
It's April, and blossom time, and white is the may;
And bright is the sun, brother, and warm is the rain,
Will ye not come home, brother, home to us again?'

It's the white road westwards is the road I must tread
To the green grass, the cool grass, and rest for heart
　　and head,
To the violets and the warm hearts and the thrushes' song,
In the fine land, the west land, the land where I belong.

John Masefield

THE TOY SHOP

WHEN I am old and pensioned and retired
   And permanently laid upon the shelf,
With nought expected of me or required,
   Wot ye how I shall occupy myself?

Not golf, not golf, for that way madness lies,
   Not books or music or the insipid joys
Of cards or chess— nay, vastly otherwise;
   I shall acquire a little shop of toys.

Toys only toys, and me and only me;
   No hireling shopmen there shall condescend;
I shall be master in my nursery,
   I shall be seller, sometimes also spend.

There shall I keep unending holiday
   Drawing delight from children's happy eyes,
And, dealing fairly, earn the right to play
   Myself of evenings with my merchandise.

And when small grubby faces at the pane
   Proclaim the envious waif, the wistful stray,
These shall be made to enter my domain,
   And shall not go unsatisfied away.

Then for myself shall follow nights of joy,
   The shutters up, a comfortable fire,
Engines and soldiers—every kind of toy,
   And mine, all mine, to play with till I tire.

The old enchantment shall again be caught
   In youthfulness of heart that setteth free
A magic rare as ever China wrought
   Or bearded djinn drew out of Araby.

Hilton Brown

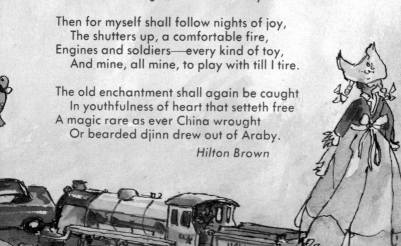

THE NIGHT WILL NEVER STAY

THE night will never stay,
  The night will still go by,
Though with a million stars
You pin it to the sky;
Though you bind it with the blowing wind
And buckle it with the moon,
The night will slip away
Like sorrow or a tune.

Eleanor Farjeon

ACKNOWLEDGMENTS

Our thanks to the Society of Authors
for "Tewkesbury Road" and "The
West Wind" by John Masefield, and
"The Night Will Never Stay" by
Eleanor Farjeon; to the Society of
Authors and Miss Pamela Hinkson
for "The Nightingale" and "The
Old Love" by Katharine Tynan; to
Methuen & Co., Ltd., for "The
Dreamer" and "The Tortoiseshell
Cat" by Patrick R. Chalmers; to Noel
Scott for "England's Weather"; to
Irene Bernaerts for "The Take
Over"; to Dorothy Margaret Paulin
for "May Song"; to Pat Lovell for
"Will You?"; to Glenda Moore
for "The Trinket Box"; to
Frances Stephens for "Lamplight";
to Charles Griffiths for "The
Adventurer" and "When We Are
Sad" by Aileen E. Passmore.